Original title:
Beyond the Dream

Copyright © 2024 Creative Arts Management OÜ
All rights reserved.

Author: Dexter Sullivan
ISBN HARDBACK: 978-9916-88-874-2
ISBN PAPERBACK: 978-9916-88-875-9

Whispers of a Distant Realm

In twilight's hush, the stars ignite,
Voices linger in the fading light.
Secrets woven in silver threads,
Carry whispers of realms long dead.

Dreams awaken on shimmering waves,
Softly calling from hidden caves.
Moonlight dances on gentle streams,
Igniting the heart with ancient dreams.

Echoes of Forgotten Visions

Shadows flicker in the misty haze,
Echoes tug at memory's gaze.
Forgotten tales of love and loss,
Carried softly, a heavy cost.

The dawn unfolds with a tender sigh,
Embers glow as time drifts by.
In the silence, a story remains,
Painted softly in shadowy veins.

The Threshold of Night's Embrace

Beneath the veil of a starry night,
Dreamers gather, hearts take flight.
A softness swells, a gentle call,
As the universe whispers to us all.

The moon hangs low, a guiding light,
Casting shadows, turning dark to bright.
In every breath, an endless chance,
To sway to the rhythm of night's dance.

In Pursuit of Celestial Lullabies

On stardust paths we softly tread,
Chasing dreams that dance overhead.
Celestial songs in the evening air,
Carry hopes and light our despair.

With every note, the cosmos sings,
Awakening love, unbinding strings.
Together we reach for the skies,
In pursuit of celestial lullabies.

Light Underneath the Shimmering Skies

Stars twinkle bright above our dreams,
Whispers of hope in moonlit beams.
Night wraps the world in a silken glow,
Guiding the heart where the cool winds blow.

Gentle breezes dance through the trees,
Soft melodies echo, a sweet, sweet tease.
Every shadow tells a tale untold,
Secrets of ages, both warm and cold.

The horizon glimmers with hues so rare,
Colors of passion that linger in air.
Beneath the vastness, our spirits sing,
Embracing the joy that each moment can bring.

In the calm of night, dreams take their flight,
Chasing the stars, igniting our light.
Together we stand, hand in hand, sublime,
In the tapestry woven by the threads of time.

A Garden of Secrets Past the Stars

In a garden where silence flows like streams,
Whispers of ancient, forgotten dreams.
Each flower blooms with a story to share,
Telling the tales of the moon's gentle care.

Amongst the petals, soft secrets hide,
Beneath the leaves, where the shadows reside.
Twilight dances on the breath of the breeze,
Stirring the memories held by the trees.

Colors collide in a painter's delight,
Creating a canvas of day turning night.
With every step, the universe sighs,
Unfolding the wonders that lie in the skies.

So linger a while in this realm so vast,
Where echoes of old intertwine with the past.
In the garden of secrets, let hearts find peace,
As the world hushes softly, and sorrows cease.

Mosaic of the Mindscape

In a realm where thoughts collide,
Ideas dance in twilight's glow.
Fragments weave a tale inside,
Crafting dreams only we know.

Colors swirl in silent streams,
Whispers echo of lost lore.
Each piece holds forgotten dreams,
A labyrinth we can't ignore.

Visions flicker, then take flight,
Boundless as the endless sky.
Every heartbeat, every sight,
Shapes our world as we comply.

Here in shadows, truths entwine,
In this mosaic, we confer.
Glimmers of a grand design,
In the silence, we infer.

The Language of Starlight

Whispers from the cosmic seas,
The stars converse in soft tones.
Galaxies sway on gentle breeze,
Drawing patterns, ancient bones.

A symphony of light and space,
Celestial notes in rhythmic flow.
In their dance, a secret trace,
A melody only few know.

Constellations paint the night,
Stories etched in luminous hues.
Each twinkle tells of endless flight,
Of worlds we ponder and peruse.

Beneath the vast celestial dome,
We listen in our hearts, awake.
The universe, our boundless home,
In starlit paths, our spirits break.

A Journey through the Vortex

Spiraling through colors bright,
A vortex pulls the dreamers in.
Lost in waves of sheer delight,
Chasing echoes where we begin.

Time and space begin to bend,
A carousel of vivid sights.
In this dance, we twist and blend,
Exploring realms of purest lights.

Fleeting moments, seconds freeze,
Captured whispers in the swirl.
Thoughts collide like autumn leaves,
In this wild and wondrous whirl.

Embraced by the cosmic tide,
We surrender, hearts alight.
In the vortex, fears subside,
As we soar into the night.

Rhapsody of the Unseen

Melodies drift in hidden spaces,
Notes that shimmer, soft and clear.
Unseen forces, gentle traces,
Harmony that draws us near.

Through the veil, we hear the song,
Echoes whisper, secrets shared.
In this rhapsody, we belong,
In the stillness, we are dared.

Hearts entwined in silent bliss,
Wrapped in warmth of thoughts and dreams.
In the void, a fleeting kiss,
Magic flows in silver beams.

As the night unveils its art,
We dance to rhythms only felt.
In the unseen, we find our heart,
In this rhapsody, we melt.

Whispers of a Distant Realm

In silent dusk, the shadows creep,
Soft echoes drift, as dreamers sleep.
Stars twinkle high, with tales untold,
A distant realm, where hearts are bold.

Whispers float on a gentle breeze,
Carrying secrets through ancient trees.
In twilight's glow, we seek the light,
Embracing mystery, we take flight.

Moonlit paths lead us far away,
Where time dissolves in a soft ballet.
Among the stars, we find our home,
In whispers soft, we freely roam.

So come, dear friend, let us explore,
This distant realm, forevermore.
With every step, our souls align,
In whispered realms, our hearts entwine.

Echoes of a Forgotten Paradise

In gardens lost to time's embrace,
Flowers bloom with gentle grace.
Echoes linger in the air,
Of laughter sweet, beyond compare.

Waves crash softly on the shore,
Whispers hint at tales of yore.
Beneath the sun's warm golden glow,
A paradise waits, where dreams can grow.

Skies painted with hues divine,
Clouds drifting like soft, spun line.
In twilight's blush, the memories rise,
Carried forth on whispered sighs.

So wander here, where time stands still,
In this paradise, feel the thrill.
For though it's forgotten, it lives anew,
In echoes soft, forever true.

Shadows of the Celestial Night

Beneath the vast and starry dome,
The night unveils its quiet home.
Shadows dance in silver light,
Whispers of the celestial night.

Galaxies spin in endless delight,
While dreams take flight in darkest night.
Among the stars, we find our way,
Guided by the moon's soft sway.

In the silence, truths unfold,
Stories woven in threads of gold.
The universe hums a timeless rhyme,
In shadows deep, we halt our climb.

So linger here, in starlit hue,
Where shadows play and visions brew.
In the celestial, our hearts ignite,
As we embrace the sacred night.

Transcendent Visions

In realms beyond our earthly gaze,
Visions dance in a vibrant haze.
Colors swirl and light cascades,
In transcendent sights, the heart invades.

Ideas flow like rivers wide,
In potential's glow, we seek to bide.
Moments fleeting, yet timeless too,
In visions pure, our spirits renew.

Awakened dreams take flight on high,
In every heartbeat, the cosmic sigh.
Within the void, we find our voice,
In transcendent realms, we make our choice.

So journey forth, embrace the light,
In visions vast, our futures bright.
With each step taken, we ignite,
The fire of hope in endless night.

Heartbeats in an Ethereal Void

In endless space where spirits glide,
Whispers linger, love won't hide.
A pulse of dreams in night's embrace,
Echoes of time in a timeless place.

Stars align with every breath,
Dancing shadows, a waltz with death.
Heartbeats synchronized in flight,
Together they fade into the light.

Reflections on a Canvas of Stars

Galaxies swirl, a painted sky,
Brush of cosmos, where wonders lie.
Each twinkle speaks of tales untold,
In silent nights, the dreams unfold.

Mirrored thoughts in stardust beams,
Reality shifts, lost in dreams.
We wander through the vast unknown,
Finding solace, never alone.

The Silent Symphony of Hope

In quiet moments, whispers play,
Notes of comfort, come what may.
A melody weaves through the dark,
Filling hearts with a gentle spark.

Each heartbeat sings a lullaby,
Promises soar, they won't deny.
Silent chords of love and light,
Guiding souls through endless night.

Threads of Light in the Darkness

Woven strands of golden grace,
Guiding us through shadowed space.
In every corner, hope will gleam,
A tapestry of every dream.

Through tangled paths, we find our way,
With every thread, we dare to stay.
In darkness' clutch, we stand anew,
Each thread a promise, bright and true.

A Symphony of the Stars

In the vastness of the night,
Stars shimmer with pure delight.
Each twinkle plays a sweet tune,
Guiding hearts to the silver moon.

Galaxies spin in a dance,
Infinite worlds in a trance.
Nebulas bloom, colors bright,
Painting dreams in the soft light.

Echoes of time whisper low,
Secrets that the heavens know.
Melodies written in the sky,
A symphony as worlds fly by.

Together, we listen wide,
To the music that won't hide.
In harmony, we will soar,
Each note calling us for more.

Dreams like Fireflies

In the twilight's gentle glow,
Fireflies flicker, soft and slow.
Whispers dance upon the breeze,
A dreamer's heart finds sweet reprise.

Each tiny light holds a wish,
Floating near on a silken swish.
Moments twinkle, fleeting, bright,
Guiding souls through the night.

They weave tales of hope and cheer,
In the dark, they draw us near.
An orchestra of gleaming sparks,
Painting pictures in the parks.

Hold your dreams with gentle grace,
Like fireflies in a warm embrace.
For in their glow, the magic lies,
In every flicker beneath the skies.

Interstellar Fantasies

Whirling in a cosmic dance,
Planets spin in a timeless trance.
Lost within the stellar glow,
Secrets of the universe flow.

Beyond the stars, our dreams expand,
In galaxies, hand in hand.
Through the void, we search and seek,
For the wonders that we speak.

Nebulae weave vibrant tales,
As starlight glimmers and sails.
Whispers echo through the night,
Of distant worlds that take flight.

In our hearts, these journeys bloom,
With every spark, dispelling gloom.
Interstellar, we shall roam,
Finding in darkness, our home.

Whispered Secrets of the Cosmos

In the silence of the dark,
Cosmic secrets leave a mark.
Stars conspire in soft whispers,
Echoing from the endless rivers.

Time bends in celestial dance,
Unraveling fate with a glance.
Each twinkle holds a story true,
Woven deep in the cosmic blue.

Mysteries of the night unfold,
As the universe dares to hold.
Every heartbeat, every sigh,
Links us to the vast, wide sky.

So listen close to the starlit breeze,
For in its depths lie truths to seize.
Whispered secrets, gentle and wise,
Guarded beneath the ancient skies.

Celestial Murmurs Through Dusk

Stars flicker softly high,
As dusk spreads her wings wide,
Secrets woven in the night,
In shadows, dreams abide.

Moonlight dances on the trees,
Whispering tales of yore,
A symphony of gentle breeze,
Crickets sing forevermore.

Beneath the velvet sky,
Hope awakens, takes flight,
In the stillness of the hour,
Our hearts ignite with light.

Time drifts like a feather,
In a cosmic ballet's sway,
Celestial murmurs linger,
Guiding souls that roam astray.

The Alchemy of A Thousand Dreams

In the forge of the mind,
Whispers of wishes collide,
Each thought a flickering flame,
In a universe vast and wide.

Shimmering visions rise,
Like phantoms in the night,
Casting shadows on the past,
Turning darkness into light.

Potions brewed with intention,
Stirred by the heart's decree,
The alchemy of creation,
Sets the restless spirit free.

Weaving threads of starlight,
Into tapestries of fate,
A thousand dreams in brilliance,
Unite in love, no hate.

Journeying through the Whispering Winds

The winds call softly here,
Guiding hearts through the trees,
They carry tales untold,
On the back of gentle breeze.

Each gust a fleeting touch,
Tepid, warm, and inviting,
Like a lover's sweet embrace,
In the twilight, delighting.

Paths unknown await ahead,
Each step a silent grace,
Journeying through whispering winds,
We find our destined place.

Nature sings with soft tones,
Symphony of the wild,
In the hush, find your voice,
Become forever a child.

The Chorus of Unfurling Fantasies

In the garden of our dreams,
Fantasies start to bloom,
Each petal holds a promise,
Banish shadows, lift the gloom.

Laughter echoes through the air,
As colors sway and weave,
A chorus of vibrant hope,
In which we all believe.

With each note, hearts awaken,
Boundless and free we soar,
The magic of our visions,
Craving evermore.

Unfurling like the blossoms,
Opening to the sun,
We dance upon the canvas,
As life's great song's begun.

Wanderlust in the Land of Reverie

In the grove where shadows dance,
Whispers call with sweet romance.
Dreamers walk on paths of light,
   Guided by the stars at night.

Every breeze brings tales anew,
Painting skies in shades of blue.
Footprints trace the heart's desire,
Igniting souls with wanderfire.

Through meadows lush and valleys deep,
Where secrets hide and thoughts dare leap.
In the land where visions blend,
Joy and magic never end.

Serendipitous Secrets of the Lost

Amidst the ruins, echoes call,
Ghosts of stories, they enthrall.
Hidden maps beneath the stone,
Whispered truths, forever lone.

With every step, a chance to find,
The secret threads of heart and mind.
Ancient whispers brush the ear,
Revealing paths once cloaked in fear.

In moonlit nights, the past awakes,
As the heartened traveler takes.
Each serendipity unveils,
The tapestry of lost details.

Maps Written in Silver Ink

A parchment spread on velvet night,
Where dreams are drawn in silver light.
Each line a journey yet untold,
Adventures waiting to unfold.

Bound by stars, our fates align,
Navigating worlds, we redefine.
With every turn, a glimpse of gold,
Stories waiting to be sold.

In hidden corners, treasures wait,
For those who dare to tempt their fate.
Maps whisper softly, hearts ignite,
Promises glow, a guiding light.

The Luminescent Veil Between Worlds

Where shadows blend with morning glow,
A veil of dreams begins to flow.
Between the realms, we drift and sway,
In twilight's arms, we find our way.

Ethereal whispers beckon near,
Bridging gaps that disappear.
In luminescent hues we fly,
As worlds entwine beneath the sky.

The edge of magic softly calls,
Inviting hearts to leap and fall.
In this embrace we lose and gain,
Through veils of light, we dance and reign.

Chasing the Fables of Tomorrow

In shadows where the stories lie,
We seek the whispers of the sky.
A tapestry of dreams unfolds,
Through paths of silver, tales of gold.

The dawn ignites with colors bright,
As visions dance in morning light.
We chase the fables, hearts on fire,
With passion's spark, we dare aspire.

Each step we take is woven fate,
A journey marked, we won't be late.
In every laugh, and every tear,
The fables whisper, drawing near.

So let us run, let spirits soar,
In search of tales forevermore.
For in the chase, we find our grace,
Chasing the fables, a boundless race.

Silhouettes of Forgotten Wishes

Beneath the stars, where shadows play,
Forgotten wishes drift away.
In corners dark, they softly sigh,
As moonlight weaves a gentle lie.

They linger in the evening breeze,
These silhouettes, like ancient trees.
With every breath, we feel their call,
Reminders sweet that love is all.

Through dreams they float, so bittersweet,
A dance of hopes, in hushed retreat.
Yet in their glow, we find the light,
Silhouettes that guide us through the night.

Hold tightly to each whispered prayer,
For every wish has left a trace.
In heart's embrace, they never fade,
Silhouettes of dreams, in twilight laid.

The Solstice of Suspended Time

In twilight's glow, the world stands still,
As time pauses, bending to will.
A moment stretched, like silent air,
We breathe the magic, unaware.

The sun dips low, a gentle kiss,
In this stillness, we find bliss.
With every heartbeat, seconds sigh,
The solstice whispers, a lullaby.

Within this space, our spirits soar,
Infinite dreams on a distant shore.
We gather whispers of the night,
In suspended time, all feels right.

So let us linger, forever here,
In this realm, where hopes are near.
For in the stillness, love will bind,
The solstice holds the peace we find.

Dreamscapes of the Untold

In realms where visions softly blend,
We wander far, no need to pretend.
Through dreamscapes vast, in colors rare,
The untold tales drift on the air.

Each whisper beckons, calling clear,
A world where doubts and fears disappear.
With every step, we carve our way,
In the fabric of night and day.

The magic swirls, like stardust bright,
Guiding us through the endless night.
In dreamscapes wild, we lose control,
Unraveling the threads of the soul.

So take my hand, let's take the leap,
Into the depths where secrets sleep.
For in these dreams, our hearts will meld,
In dreamscapes wide, the joy unveiled.

Chasing the Horizon

Feet rush forward, the sun dips low,
A path of gold in the evening's glow.
Endless skies call, a whisper so sweet,
Each step a promise, new worlds to greet.

The breeze carries tales of distant lands,
With open hearts and outstretched hands.
Waves crash softly on shores unknown,
In chase of the horizon, we roam alone.

Mountains loom like giants in the mist,
In shadows deep, new dreams persist.
The edge of night, a canvas wide,
Where moments freeze, and time abides.

Stars awake, like fireflies in flight,
Guiding our souls through the velvet night.
With hope as our compass, we'll find our way,
Chasing the horizon, come what may.

Through the Mists of Dream

In shadows soft, the night unfolds,
Whispers of wonders, mysteries untold.
Velvet skies cradle the timid stars,
Guiding our hearts through night's open bars.

Through mists of dream, we wander light,
Veils of silence envelop the night.
Each step we take on the ethereal ground,
Where echoes of dreams are tenderly found.

Golden fragments of wishes long cast,
Carried by breezes through hours past.
Time melts like silver, a river so wide,
In the realm of dreams, we drift and glide.

Awake or asleep, where do we stand?
In a dance with shadows, hand in hand.
Through the mists, we'll forever roam,
For in dreams, we'll always find home.

Portraits of a Moonlit Evening

Under silver light, the world transforms,
Quiet whispers wrap, in gentle swarms.
Canvas stretched wide, the night paints clear,
Each brushstroke a story we hold dear.

Trees like statues in the soft glow lie,
With branches dancing, reaching for the sky.
The river reflects a shimmering tale,
Where secrets of night and memory sail.

In stillness, the night breathes a sigh,
Portraits of moments, where memories lie.
With every flicker, the stars align,
Orchestrating dreams, a celestial design.

In the hush of dusk, we find our grace,
In every shadow, we see a face.
Through the moonlit veil, our hearts unite,
Portraits captured in the gentle night.

Fading Echoes of Eternity

Whispers linger in the twilight air,
Fading echoes of a world laid bare.
Time trickles slow, like a gentle stream,
Carving the silence of a half-remembered dream.

In the distance, shadows blend and sway,
Memories drift, like leaves in a ballet.
Each heartbeat a rhythm of the past,
Where echoes of eternity steadfast.

Stars flicker softly, like candles aglow,
In the canvas of night, their secrets flow.
Fragile moments, like whispers of light,
Guide us through the depths of the night.

As dawn approaches, the echoes fade,
Yet in our souls, their warmth cascades.
In the whisper of time, we find our way,
Fading echoes, in our hearts, they'll stay.

Pathways through the Aether

In the hush where silence weaves,
Whispers find their gentle leaves.
Stars ignite in cosmic flight,
Guiding souls through endless night.

Winding trails of stardust bright,
Silver threads in darkened light.
Celestial winds call our name,
In a dance of fate and flame.

Beyond the veil where shadows blend,
Timeless echoes never end.
Every step a spark of grace,
Navigating endless space.

Fingers trace the unseen lines,
Mapping dreams in sacred signs.
Together we discover truth,
In the pathways of our youth.

Reflections in a Cosmic Mirror

Gaze upon the endless night,
Galaxies in swirling flight.
Mirrored realms of light and shade,
Fleeting moments softly laid.

Time unwinds in distant hues,
Infinite, the paths we choose.
In the stillness find the spark,
Every echo leaves its mark.

Voices rise from stardust past,
Whispered tales that forever last.
In the depths of silence ring,
Reflections of the heart take wing.

Journey deep into the soul,
Where the cosmic forces roll.
In this mirror of the skies,
We discover who we are, our ties.

The Heart of the Universe

In the pulse of stardust light,
A rhythm echoes through the night.
Every heartbeat tells a tale,
Of dreams that soar and hopes that sail.

Galaxies spin with tender grace,
Holding secrets in their space.
Infinite love in cosmic sway,
Guiding us through night and day.

With every breath, the cosmos sings,
A melody of timeless things.
In the quiet, feel the flame,
The heart of the universe is the same.

Together, we are intertwined,
A symphony of the divine.
Fates woven in threads of gold,
A story of the brave and bold.

Sailing the Sea of Dreams

Drifting on the moonlit waves,
Where the heart of silence braves.
Every star a guiding light,
On this journey through the night.

Clouds like sails in twilight's breeze,
Whispers carried through the trees.
In the depths of azure seas,
Hope and wonder find their keys.

Navigating worlds unseen,
On the canvas where we dream.
Every thought a billowed sail,
In the winds that softly trail.

Sailing forth on dreams anew,
Every moment feels so true.
In this vastness, we find peace,
As the sea of dreams won't cease.

Fragments of a Dreamscape

In twilight's grasp, shadows dance slow,
Whispers of realms where lost echoes flow.
Colors collide in surreal embrace,
A tapestry woven, a dreamlike space.

Fleeting glimpses of memories fade,
Beneath silver stars, a new path is laid.
Time loses meaning, and silence prevails,
As heartbeats echo in ethereal trails.

Faces of strangers, yet known so well,
Each moment a story, each sigh a spell.
Drifting on clouds made of soft twilight,
In fragments of dreams, we take flight.

Awake or asleep? The line blurs and bends,
In dreamscape fragments, where the journey never ends.

Chasing Celestial Gleams

Upon the hilltop, where night birds soar,
I seek the stars, forevermore.
With every whisper of the cosmic breeze,
I chase the glimmers that dance with ease.

Galaxies spin in a timeless ballet,
While constellations guide me along the way.
In the dark canvas, a painter's delight,
Each distant dot, a lost dream ignites.

Stardust falls softly like dreams unspun,
Illuminating paths where shadows run.
In the vast silence, a heartbeat I find,
Chasing celestial gleams, unconfined.

With eyes wide open, I reach for the skies,
In pursuit of the light, where possibility lies.

The Universe Within

Deep in the stillness, a spark ignites,
A universe swirling, in quiet delights.
Hidden within, a vast ocean flows,
Endless horizons where wonder surely grows.

Thoughts intertwine like celestial threads,
Weaving the fabric where imagination treads.
In every heartbeat, a new world appears,
The universe whispers, erasing our fears.

Mirrors of moments cascade through the mind,
Galaxies born from the fabric we find.
In the depths of our souls, the starlight may spin,
Discovering wonders, the universe within.

Awake in the night, dreamers take flight,
Exploring the realms where the stars feel right.

Enigmas of the Ethereal

In the misty shadows, secrets take form,
Enigmas dance gently, a whispering storm.
Veils of illusion wrap softly around,
Where questions unravel and answers abound.

Time bends and twists in a delicate waltz,
Chasing the echoes of forgotten faults.
In realms of the unseen, silence sings low,
Unlocking the wonders that only night knows.

Glimmers of truth flicker, then fade,
Shifting like sand through the hands of the fayed.
In every heartbeat, the cosmos does call,
Enigmas of the ethereal, binding us all.

We wander through whispers, through twilight and dreams,
Seeking the magic in all that redeems.

A Universe of Hopes

Stars whisper softly in the night,
Each flicker a wish, a glimmer of light.
In this vast space, dreams start to rise,
Floating like doves, towards hopeful skies.

Galaxies gleam with stories untold,
Every heartbeat a wish, a future to hold.
Among cosmic winds, aspirations soar,
Each pulse a reminder: there's always more.

The moon guides us through shadows and fear,
Casting silver beams to make paths clear.
In the silence, we dare to believe,
In a universe where hearts can achieve.

Among the dust of the worlds that gleam,
We find our strength in every dream.
A tapestry woven with love and grace,
In this universe, there's always a place.

The Poetry of Whimsy

In gardens where laughter grows bright,
Whimsical wonders dance in the light.
Butterflies giggle, flowers sway,
In this world, the playful find their way.

With each silly rhyme, a joy is found,
In the magic of moments that spin around.
Clouds wear hats, the sun wears a grin,
In this realm of charm, let the fun begin.

Puppies chase rainbows, kittens on trees,
Every leaf whispers secrets to the breeze.
In the poetry of whimsy, we roam,
Finding our joy, wherever we call home.

So let your spirit take flight and sing,
Embrace the delight that each day can bring.
In laughter and light, let your heart play,
In the poetry of whimsy, come out and stay.

A Canvas of Endless Dreams

Colors collide on the canvas wide,
Where visions emerge, where hopes reside.
Brushstrokes of courage, splashes of grace,
Creating a world, a beautiful space.

Each hue tells a tale, each shade sings a song,
Of the dreams that gather, where hearts belong.
In the silence of magic, inspiration flows,
Filling the canvas where imagination glows.

Wonders awaken in every stroke,
Whispers of dreams, unbound and bespoke.
As layers unfold, possibilities teem,
On this canvas, we paint our dream.

So dip your brush in dreams untold,
Create your story, let life unfold.
In hues of passion, let fate redeem,
On this canvas, we live our dream.

Navigating the Cosmic Ocean

Sailing on tides of shimmering night,
Stars like beacons, guiding our flight.
The cosmos stretches, mysterious and wide,
In this ocean of dreams, we take every stride.

Planets spin gently, an elegant dance,
Whispers of wonder, they enhance our chance.
Through stardust and light, we chart our way,
Navigating the cosmos, seizing the day.

Comets trail stories, their paths ignite,
Each journey a tale, a flicker of light.
Eclipses and phases, the beauty we find,
In this grand voyage, we're intertwined.

So grab the helm, let your spirit soar,
In the cosmic ocean, there's always more.
With eyes on the stars, hearts full of ambition,
We navigate dreams with purposeful vision.

Ascent into the Unknown

Upward I climb, through shadows and mist,
The path unwinds, a daring twist.
Whispers of fate guide my way,
Into the depths of a brand new day.

Each step I take, a heartbeat's song,
With courage bestowed, I must be strong.
The air is thick with dreams untold,
Embracing the chill, I feel the bold.

Mountains loom high, the summit calls,
In silence I rise, where wonder falls.
Clouds weave tales as old as time,
In this ascent, I seek to climb.

The unknown awaits, a realm so wide,
With faith as my compass, I shall abide.
Beyond the horizon, the future awaits,
As I journey forth, destiny creates.

Embracing the Light

In twilight's grace, the shadows fade,
I lift my face where hope is laid.
Golden rays pierce through the dark,
Awakening dreams with their spark.

The warmth surrounds, a soft embrace,
Each beam a guide, a sacred space.
I shed my fears, let go of night,
With open arms, I embrace the light.

Nature sings in vibrant hues,
A symphony born from morning's dues.
With every dawn, a chance to see,
The beauty that blooms, setting me free.

We dance in joy, souls intertwined,
With every heartbeat, love defined.
Together we'll shine, a radiant sight,
For in our hearts, we hold the light.

Secrets of the Night Sky

The stars whisper secrets, ancient and wise,
Glimmers of stories in the velvet skies.
A tapestry spun with silken thread,
Guiding the dreamers, the lost, the led.

As constellations twinkle in silent grace,
I find my thoughts in this endless space.
Planets parade in celestial dance,
Inviting my spirit to take a chance.

Moonlight cascades, a silver plume,
Filling the night with a soft perfume.
Each shadowed corner holds tales untold,
In mysteries woven, so fragile, so bold.

So I gaze up high, my heart takes flight,
In the serene embrace of this tranquil night.
For in the darkness, the truths reveal,
The secrets of the sky that time can't conceal.

Celestial Callings

A voice from above, celestial and clear,
Calls to the wanderers, drawing them near.
Echoes of truth across spacetime we trace,
In the grand tapestry of boundless grace.

Galaxies swirl in a cosmic embrace,
Each star a beacon, a sacred place.
Infinite realms beckon with light,
As we embark on this endless flight.

With every heartbeat, we shift and we soar,
Through nebulas bright, to horizons galore.
Chasing the whispers of faraway spheres,
We dance with the cosmos, transcending our fears.

Forever we yearn for the unknown embrace,
In the vastness of space, we find our place.
Celestial callings, profound and bright,
In the journey of souls, we ignite the night.

Celestial Reveries

Stars whisper secrets in the night,
A dance of dreams in soft moonlight.
Galaxies beckon with endless grace,
In their embrace, we find our place.

Wonders unfold in the cosmic sea,
Timeless tales of what's yet to be.
Comets trail with a shimmering gleam,
Guiding the lost through a starlit dream.

Nebulas glow with colors untold,
In their warmth, the mysteries unfold.
Planets spin in a celestial waltz,
Each orbit a story, each arc, a pulse.

In the quiet of space, our hearts align,
We breathe in the echoes of the divine.
Through the vastness, we drift and glide,
In celestial reveries, forever we ride.

In the Embrace of Illusion

Mirages dance on the desert sand,
Whispers of dreams held in our hand.
Veils of mist shroud the path we tread,
In the embrace of illusion, we are led.

The world spins in colors so bright,
Reality bends in the fading light.
What is truth when shadows play?
In illusions, we find our way.

Chasing visions that flicker and fade,
Life, a tapestry intricately laid.
Moments glimmer like stars in the sea,
In the embrace of illusion, we are free.

Yet beneath the surface, a pulse does thrive,
In the heart of delusion, we feel alive.
With every breath, we weave our design,
In the embrace of illusion, we intertwine.

Odyssey of the Unseen

Whispers of journeys in shadows reside,
Paths untraveled, where secrets abide.
Footsteps echo in echoes of time,
An odyssey waits without reason or rhyme.

Through hidden valleys and forests deep,
The unseen beckons, a promise to keep.
Veiled horizons, the dawns yet to claim,
In silence, we chase the elusive flame.

Mountains rise like dreams yet untold,
In the tapestry woven, our fates unfold.
With each heartbeat, the call grows strong,
In the odyssey of the unseen, we belong.

Guided by starlight and whispers of fate,
In realms beyond, we contemplate.
Our spirits soar on wings of the rare,
In the odyssey of the unseen, we dare.

Beyond the Veil of Sleep

In the twilight where shadows creep,
Dreams awaken beyond the veil of sleep.
Stars wink softly, inviting the night,
Guiding the way with their gentle light.

Winds of fantasy whisper and roam,
Carrying souls to a distant home.
In hidden lands, where the heart is free,
Beyond the veil, we find the key.

Mountains of wonder rise in the dark,
Illuminated softly by a fleeting spark.
Through the corridors of the night we glide,
In the embrace of dreams, we confide.

Awake or asleep, the line blurs near,
In the realm of slumber, nothing to fear.
With every breath, our stories weave,
Beyond the veil of sleep, we believe.

The Fountain of Illusions

In gardens where whispers softly play,
Shadows dance, leading hearts astray.
Mirrored waters reflect the dreams,
Crafting truths from silent schemes.

Petals float on a gentle breeze,
Carrying secrets through the trees.
A sip from the fountain, sweet and bold,
Reveals a world of glimmering gold.

Every drop, a story unfurled,
In the depths of this wondrous world.
Reality bends, loses its way,
In the fountain where illusions play.

With every moment, truth may bend,
The tales we weave must never end.
So linger here, take your time,
For in this dream, everything shall rhyme.

Timeless Reveries

In the hush of the fading light,
Whispers of yesterdays take flight.
Echoes of laughter fill the air,
Carried on dreams, beyond all care.

Time stands still in this sacred space,
Where memories wander at a gentle pace.
Moments linger, like a sigh,
In the timeless realm where we fly.

Stars blink softly in the night,
Guiding lost souls to the light.
Each twinkle speaks of countless tales,
Of love and loss that never pales.

So close your eyes, let visions roam,
For in these dreams, you are home.
Together we soar, through time and space,
In these timeless reveries, we find our place.

Surfing on the Waves of Wonder

Catch the cresting wave with a grin,
Ride the thrill, let the journey begin.
Oceans shimmer in the golden hue,
Embrace the vastness, feel the blue.

Each swell tells tales of the deep,
Where mermaids dance and secrets sleep.
The surfboard glides, a seamless glide,
Bringing joy with every tide.

Beneath the sun, the world spins bright,
In the hands of wonder, pure delight.
A splash of spray, a wave's embrace,
In this dance, we find our place.

Ride the rhythm of the ocean's song,
In the heart of wonder, we belong.
Surfing on dreams, with spirits high,
Forever free, we touch the sky.

Celestial Cartography

Gaze upon the tapestry of stars,
Mapping dreams from Venus to Mars.
Constellations whisper secrets old,
In the night sky, wonders unfold.

Navigators of the cosmic seas,
Charting paths with the softest breeze.
Each twinkle, a beacon, guiding our way,
In this celestial ballet, we sway.

Drawn by the moon, we follow its light,
Through dreams that shimmer in the night.
A compass of hope, in the vast unknown,
In the cosmos, we've truly grown.

So let the cosmos unveil its art,
For in the stars, we find our heart.
Celestial cartography, our souls aligned,
In the grand design, love is defined.

Dreaming in Color

In a world where wishes soar,
Painted skies and oceans roar,
Whispers of a vibrant hue,
Every dream, a glimpse of you.

Colors dance on golden dawn,
In the twilight, dreams are drawn,
With each brushstroke, hope ignites,
Dreams take flight on starry nights.

Through the canvas, stories flow,
In each shade, our spirits grow,
Every heartbeat, a new design,
In this realm, your hand in mine.

Wake me not from such delight,
Let me dream through endless night,
Each moment a swirling art,
In this color, find my heart.

Clarity at the Edge of Clouds

Above the fray, where silence reigns,
Clouds disperse, dissolving chains,
In the stillness, insight gleams,
Whispers of forgotten dreams.

Bathed in light, the truth appears,
Shadows fade, dissolving fears,
Every thought like feathers tossed,
In this peace, no vision lost.

With each breath, clarity glows,
Nature's pulse, the wisdom flows,
As I stand on heaven's brink,
I discover, I can think.

As the world beneath me spins,
In this moment, life begins,
At the edge, I find my way,
Clarity in light of day.

Vistas of the Uncharted

Footsteps echo on the ground,
In the wilds, new sights are found,
Mountains rise like ancient lore,
Every shadow, secrets store.

As I wander through the trees,
Whispers carried by the breeze,
Paths untraveled, spirits call,
In the vastness, I stand tall.

Wonders hide in every nook,
Nature's pages, open book,
With each turn, a treasure seeks,
In these vistas, silence speaks.

Uncharted realms, a tale begins,
Where adventure lies within,
In the journey, freedom's spark,
In the light, I leave my mark.

Echoing Nightfall

As the sun dips below the trees,
Night enfolds with tender ease,
Stars awaken, softly bright,
In the hush, the world takes flight.

Moonlight dances on the waves,
Whispers rise from hidden caves,
Every echo, softly calls,
In the dark, a mystery falls.

Shadows drift and shadows play,
Night's embrace, a warm ballet,
Voices linger on the air,
In this silence, love lays bare.

As the clock counts down the hours,
Dreams unfold like fragrant flowers,
Echoing through night's deep thrall,
In the dark, we're one and all.

Dreams in a Kaleidoscope

In a swirl of colors bright,
Visions dance in playful flight,
Shifting shapes, oh, what delight,
Night unfolds its glowing light.

Whispers of a world unseen,
Where the wild and wanderers glean,
Chasing shadows, soft and keen,
In the space where dreams have been.

Hope's embrace in fractured hue,
Each fragment holds a story true,
In the depths, a spark anew,
Life refracted, fresh and blue.

So let the night unfold its charms,
With every twist, the heart warms,
In kaleidoscopic arms,
A universe that gently calms.

Elysian Whispers

Soft as dawn's first kiss of light,
Echoes weave through morning bright,
Caressing ears with sweet delight,
In the hush of day's birthright.

Gentle breezes carry tales,
Of ancient lands and whispered gales,
Where every leaf in silence sails,
In harmony, the heart prevails.

Mystic voices, low and clear,
Invite the wandering soul near,
To dance among the stars so dear,
In Elysium, all is near.

The sun dips low, a golden thread,
While shadows stretch, the day is fed,
In twilight's glow, the heart has bled,
Yet finds its peace when softly read.

Threads of Cosmic Mystery

In the silence of the night,
Stars weave tales, the cosmos bright,
With every twinkle, a spark ignites,
In the fabric of eternal flight.

Woven dreams of distant spheres,
Catch the whispers of our fears,
Lighting paths through cosmic years,
Binding hearts as fate endears.

Galaxies dance, a choreographed art,
While the universe plays its part,
Each thread a note, a beating heart,
In the silence, we find our start.

So let us gaze into the night,
Embrace the wonder, take delight,
In every thread that shines so bright,
Cosmic tales in endless flight.

A Tapestry of Lost Tales

In the shadows, stories hide,
Whispers of those who lived and died,
Threads of memory, intertwined,
Tales of love and hearts denied.

Each stitch a moment, rich and rare,
Binding dreams with solemn care,
In fabric worn, emotions share,
Legacies in the quiet air.

Echoes of laughter, tears that fall,
A tapestry that holds them all,
Captured in the weaver's call,
A chronicle of rise and fall.

So delve into these woven seams,
Explore the shadows of forgotten dreams,
In the tapestry, life gleams,
A patchwork of lost and sacred themes.

Realms of Infinite Wonder

In gardens where the wild blooms sway,
Whispers of magic dance and play,
Stars twinkle in the velvet sky,
Time stands still as dreams drift by.

A river of colors flows like dreams,
Reflecting the sun's golden beams,
Mountains rise to kiss the clouds,
Nature speaks, gentle and loud.

Hidden paths lead to secrets untold,
Adventures await, both brave and bold,
Every shadow holds a tale,
Where courage blooms and fears grow pale.

In realms where enchantment resides,
Explore the world where wonder abides,
Infinite joys in every sigh,
A tapestry woven as time slips by.

The Edge of the Enchanted

At the edge of the forest's heart,
Where magic and mystery never part,
Ancient oaks whisper stories of old,
Their leaves shimmer with a glimmer of gold.

Moonlit paths beckon the brave,
With secrets hidden in every cave,
Echoes of laughter, soft as the breeze,
In this enchanted world, all hearts find ease.

Fairy lights twinkle in the night,
Guiding dreamers with gentle light,
Every step leads to a new delight,
In realms where day gives way to night.

Here, wishes are made with a single sigh,
In the silence, hear the spirits nigh,
The edge of the enchanted, a doorway wide,
Where magic and dreams forever abide.

Flights of Fancy

High above on wings of glee,
Imagination sets us free,
Clouds become castles painted bright,
In the canvas of the endless night.

Whirling through the skies we soar,
Exploring lands with tales galore,
Each thought a feather, light and grand,
As we sketch our dreams in the sand.

With every heartbeat, stories unfold,
A tapestry of wonder to behold,
Adventurous souls in gardens of time,
Dancing with stars in a realm sublime.

Flights of fancy, bold and bright,
In realms where daydreams take their flight,
Together we'll wander, explore, and weave,
A world of magic, with hearts that believe.

Where Imagination Soars

In realms where thoughts can take to flight,
Imagination turns darkness to light,
A canvas vast, with colors aflame,
Each stroke a whisper, calling your name.

Through forests thick with ancient lore,
Adventures await behind every door,
With every echo, hear the call,
In a world where wishes can never fall.

Dreams like butterflies spread their wings,
In the garden of hope, where joy sings,
Chasing the sun on rivers of air,
Finding magic in moments rare.

Where imagination knows no bounds,
In every heartbeat, a melody sounds,
Unleash your spirit, let it roam,
In this beautiful realm, you'll find your home.

Journey through the Starry Abyss

In the dark we wander free,
Among the stars, a tapestry,
Galaxies whisper, secrets vast,
Time dissolves, the die is cast.

Nebulas swirl, colors bright,
Infinite dreams explode in flight,
Gravity's pull, a gentle guide,
In this void, we shall confide.

Comets blaze a trail of gold,
Stories of the brave and bold,
In the cosmos, we'll find our way,
Chasing dawn, forever sway.

Each star a fire, a beacon's call,
Together we rise, together we fall,
Through the abyss, our spirits soar,
Journeying on, forevermore.

The Veil Between Worlds

In twilight's hush, the shadows creep,
Awakening secrets, buried deep,
A whisper of magic, soft and sweet,
Where realms converge, and spirits meet.

Through the mist, I see you there,
A spectral dance in the cool night air,
The veil is thin, the magic stirs,
Between these worlds, our essence purrs.

Silent echoes of tales untold,
In this liminal space, dreams unfold,
Threads of fate woven tight,
Weaving the day into the night.

With every breath, the barrier fades,
In the heart of dusk, where hope cascades,
Here we stand, on destiny's line,
In the glow of worlds, intertwine.

Beneath the Luminous Skies

Underneath a blanket vast,
Stars like diamonds, shadows cast,
Whispers of the night surround,
In nature's cradle, peace is found.

The moon ascends, a silver queen,
Guiding dreams that softly glean,
Each twinkle tells a story true,
Of distant lands and skies so blue.

Crickets serenade the dusk,
While fragrant blooms release their musk,
A gentle breeze begins to weave,
A tapestry of what we believe.

Beneath this glowing, endless dome,
We find our hearts, we find our home,
In the night's embrace, so bold,
Together, we write tales of old.

Awakening in the Twilight

As daylight fades, a soft embrace,
The sky ignites, a painted space,
With hues of orange, pink, and blue,
Awakening whispers, fresh and new.

The stars emerge, a silent song,
In twilight's grasp, where dreams belong,
Each heartbeat echoes, deep and clear,
In the stillness, love draws near.

Beneath the glow of fading light,
Possibilities take wondrous flight,
In shadows cast, our hopes arise,
A symphony beneath the skies.

Awakened souls, we seek and find,
A world transformed, an open mind,
In twilight's glow, we dance and sway,
Awakening dreams, come what may.

Astral Connections

In the silence of the night, we soar,
Boundless spirits forevermore.
Stars whisper secrets in the dark,
Guiding hearts with a gentle spark.

Through the veils of time we weave,
Invisible threads that never leave.
Every dream a tender tie,
Linking souls that touch the sky.

In the cosmic dance we find,
Echoes of the heart and mind.
Celestial voices call us near,
In this space, we feel no fear.

Fading into the midnight hue,
Together, old and yet so new.
In harmony, we softly blend,
An astral bond that has no end.

Lullabies of the Soul

Hush now, let the twilight sing,
Sweetest dreams are on the wing.
Softly drift, the stars align,
In the stillness, hearts entwine.

Whispers woven in the breeze,
Bathe in night's embrace with ease.
Every sigh, a soothing balm,
In this moment, pure and calm.

Cradled in the moon's soft light,
Wander through the gentle night.
Time stands still, a tender hush,
In the quiet, feel the rush.

Close your eyes and let them roam,
Find the way back to your home.
Lullabies of love so deep,
Grant us peace as we softly sleep.

Portals to Another Realm

In shadows cast by candle glow,
Mysteries begin to flow.
With a breath, we step beyond,
Into realms where dreams respond.

Whirling paths of light we trace,
Finding solace in this space.
Every heartbeat, a new door,
Guiding us to evermore.

Through the veil, the echoes call,
In this journey, we stand tall.
Stars above, a map we see,
Portals to eternity.

Join the dance of what is real,
Every moment, hearts reveal.
In this magic, we transcend,
To the places without end.

Footprints on the Astral Map

Each step we take upon the night,
Leaves a trace of purest light.
Whispers of our souls remain,
Guiding others through the pain.

Footprints glimmer, softly glowed,
In the silence, stories flowed.
Every echo marks the past,
Memories in stardust cast.

Through the cosmos, paths unwind,
In the tapestry, we find.
Journeys shared, no road alone,
In the universe, we've grown.

With every star that lights the way,
We discover more each day.
Grateful for the map we trace,
Footprints in the vast embrace.

Driftwood Hearts on Starlit Seas

On waves of whispers, we drift apart,
Where time stands still, and dreams restart.
With hearts like driftwood, weathered and worn,
We search for solace in tales reborn.

Beneath the starlit canopy, we lay,
Promises linger like the dawn's soft grey.
Each shimmering glimmer, a moment held tight,
Guiding our souls through the endless night.

Yet tides will turn, and currents will pull,
Carrying echoes of love, bittersweet and full.
In the ocean's breath, we find our way,
Drifting together, come what may.

As we sail through shadows, hand in hand,
Our driftwood hearts, anchored in the sand.
Together we roam, beneath the moon's glow,
On starlit seas where wild dreams flow.

The Echoes of Midnight's Promise

In the still of night, whispers unfold,
Stories of dreams, both timid and bold.
Under silver skies, we chase the unseen,
Hearing the echoes of what might have been.

Stars twinkle softly, secrets they share,
In the void of darkness, we cast away care.
With every heartbeat, a promise is made,
To cherish the night where our fears fade.

The moon stands witness to vows unbroken,
In the silence, our love is spoken.
We dance with shadows, our spirits entwined,
Bound by the magic that only night finds.

Yet as dawn approaches, whispers grow faint,
But midnight's promise, we carry, a saint.
For every ending births a new start,
In the echoing depths of our faithful hearts.

A Journey Through Unseen Horizons

Across the valleys of dreams untold,
We wander through shadows, brave and bold.
With the compass of hope, we chart our way,
Through unseen horizons, we seize the day.

Mountains loom high, wrapped in misty grace,
Every step forward, a daring embrace.
In the whispers of wind, we hear our call,
A journey of souls, where we rise or fall.

Over rivers of doubt, we carefully tread,
With courage as our armor, fears left unsaid.
The horizon beckons, an alluring glow,
With each new dawn, our spirits will grow.

For in this journey, together we find,
The beauty of life, with courage aligned.
On the path unknown, we will leave our mark,
In the tapestry woven, we ignite the spark.

Threads of Illusion in the Moonlight

In the moonlight's glow, illusions unfurl,
A dance of shadows in a mystic whirl.
Threads entwined in the fabric of night,
We chase the mirage, seeking the light.

With every glimmer, a tale to compose,
In the twilight's embrace, our fantasy grows.
We weave our secrets in silken strands,
Lost in the magic of unseen lands.

Yet the dawn will break, the veil will lift,
Revealing the truth in this delicate gift.
But for now, we revel in dreams' sweet bite,
Threads of illusion in the enchanting night.

As the stars dim slowly, we hold on tight,
To the dreams we crafted, a wondrous sight.
In the heart of the night, our spirits ignite,
In threads of illusion, we take flight.

Shadows of What Could Have Been

In the quiet corners of my mind,
Shadows dance, lost yet defined.
Echoes whisper of paths untaken,
Fading dreams, slowly forsaken.

Moments linger, a fragile thread,
What ifs plaguing all I've said.
The choices made, the doors shut tight,
Leaving ghosts in the fading light.

A tapestry woven with silent sighs,
Stories etched in starlit skies.
Yet here I dwell, with heart that's torn,
In the shadows, I'm reborn.

Every glance a fleeting chance,
Life's cruel twist, a haunting dance.
But in these shadows, wisdom grew,
A beauty found in what I knew.

Navigate the Starlit Abyss

Beneath the canvas of cosmic night,
Stars ignite with distant light.
A voyage starts, through dreams I glide,
In the starlit abyss, I confide.

Waves of silence, whispers of fate,
Each twinkle beckons, pulling me straight.
Galaxies swirl in a mystic flight,
Navigating through the cosmic bite.

Infinite wonders, so vast and wide,
Unraveled secrets, like an endless tide.
With every breath, I chase the glow,
In the starlit abyss, my heart learns to flow.

Floating onward, where dreams align,
Mapping trails across the divine.
Among the stars, I find my place,
In the endless void, I embrace the space.

Kaleidoscope of Unraveled Fantasies

In a world of colors, bright and bold,
Each twist reveals stories untold.
A kaleidoscope, spinning dreams anew,
Where fantasies dance like morning dew.

Fragments of hope in vibrant array,
Shaping visions that lead the way.
Mirrors reflecting what could be true,
In this tapestry, shades of you.

Each turn a journey, a glimpse of desire,
Sparkling moments fueled by fire.
Through the lens of wonder, I glide,
In a kaleidoscope, I will abide.

Embracing the chaos, letting life flow,
In the swirl of enchantment, I grow.
Bathed in colors, laughter and glee,
A world alive, forever free.

The Enigmatic Path of Sleep

In twilight's hush, the whispers call,
To the enigmatic path where shadows fall.
A tranquil realm where dreams reside,
In the depths of night, I slip and glide.

Stars may flicker in the velvet dark,
Guiding wayfarers to embark.
Each slumber beckons, a beckoning hand,
To wander the landscapes, unplanned.

Through hazy valleys, time stands still,
In the stillness, the faintest thrill.
With every breath, I drift away,
On the enigmatic path, I sway.

What secrets lie beneath the veil?
In whispers of night, these dreams prevail.
Embracing the magic, serene and deep,
I surrender gently to the realm of sleep.

Meditations at the Horizon

In the quiet dawn, the sky alights,
A canvas brushed with golden sights.
Waves of whispers in the breeze,
Softly carry dreams with ease.

Horizons blend with thoughts so deep,
Awakening visions that gently seep.
In stillness, I find my way,
Guided by the break of day.

Each breath a moment, each sigh a gift,
As time's currents around me shift.
With eyes wide open, I embrace,
The beauty found in every place.

A journey within, a heart set free,
Finding peace in what will be.
In the distance, hope does sing,
And in my soul, new colors spring.

When Stars Collide

In the velvet night, a spark ignites,
Two stars entwined in cosmic flights.
A dance of light that twirls and beams,
Creating magic from our dreams.

Collision fierce, yet beauty born,
From chaos, paths of light are worn.
Galaxies whisper, secrets shared,
In the depths, our souls are bared.

In intense embrace, we break apart,
Expanding realms, a brand new start.
Fleeting moments, oh so bright,
Illuminate the endless night.

As worlds collide, in silence, we find,
A union of the heart and mind.
Among the shadows, we arise,
In love and stardust, we are wise.

Whispers of the Infinite

In the hush of night, secrets flow,
Whispers of time, like rivers, grow.
Threads unspun, yet tightly wound,
In silence, the answers are found.

Echoes of dreams in twilight's fold,
Ancient stories waiting to be told.
In the vastness, a gentle guide,
Reminds us where our hopes abide.

Light cascades through the cosmic veil,
Carrying visions that do not pale.
Each moment a flicker, a breath, a pause,
In the dance of existence, we find our cause.

In the infinite, all hearts align,
Whispers of love through the corridors shine.
Together we wander, together we seek,
In the realm of the boundless, we find what's unique.

Glimpses of Forgotten Landscapes

Through the mists of time, shadows play,
Glimpses of lands that drift away.
Ancient trees with stories to tell,
In whispers soft, they weave their spell.

Cascading rivers, a gentle sigh,
Holding the laughter of days gone by.
Mountains cradling the skies so wide,
Guarding the secrets that they abide.

Fields of wildflowers, colors so bright,
Stretching towards the fading light.
Each petal a memory, soft and sweet,
Echoing tales where past and present meet.

As day embraces the night's cool breath,
I wander through the echoes of death.
In these landscapes of what was before,
I find my heart yearning for more.

Milton Keynes UK
Ingram Content Group UK Ltd.
UKHW030750121124
451094UK00013B/799